A WINDOW ON WILLIAMSBURG

A Window on Williamsburg

Photographs by TAYLOR LEWIS, JR.

Text by JOHN J. WALKLET, JR.
THOMAS K. FORD
and
DONNA C. SHEPPARD

THE COLONIAL WILLIAMSBURG FOUNDATION
Williamsburg, Virginia

© 1983
by The Colonial Williamsburg Foundation
SECOND REVISED EDITION, FOURTH PRINTING, 1987

Previous editions copyright 1966, 1973, 1975

Hardbound edition distributed by Holt, Rinehart and
    Winston, New York, N.Y.
Distributed simultaneously in Canada by Holt, Rinehart
    and Winston of Canada, Limited

Library of Congress Cataloging in Publication Data

Lewis, Taylor Biggs.
    A window on Williamsburg.

    1. Williamsburg (Va.)—Description—Views.
I. Walklet, John J., 1922-   . II. Ford, Thomas K.
III. Title.
F234.W7L4   1983   975.5'4252'00222   82-23596
ISBN 0-87935-072-5
ISBN 0-87935-071-7 (pbk.)

Printed in the United States of America

BRIGHT as the gold that lured adventurers to the New World, a
dandelion thrusts its shaggy head above the gnarled roots of a
Williamsburg tree. Just as it flowered in this unlikely spot, so the seed
of English settlement planted at Jamestown blossomed on the edge of
the wilderness. Transplanted to Williamsburg after nearly a century,
the seedling of empire flourished here.

Williamsburg was one of the most important training grounds for
the leaders of American independence. For eighty-one years (1699–
1780) it was Virginia's colonial and state capital, a political and cultural
center that ranked in importance with Boston, Philadelphia, Newport,
Charleston, Annapolis, and New York. Here George Washington,
Patrick Henry, George Wythe, Thomas Jefferson, George Mason, and
other patriots helped to shape the foundations of our government.

The prosperous little city those great men knew is the one we see
today, restored to its appearance in the years before and during the
Revolution. The preservation project, inspired by Dr. W. A. R.
Goodwin and launched in 1926 with the guidance and support of
John D. Rockefeller, Jr., continues under the supervision of the
Colonial Williamsburg Foundation, a publicly supported foundation.

Overleaf:
The Palace fish pond or "canal"
with its chinoiserie footbridge.

A little girl's garden needs a fence . . .

for little birds to perch upon

. . . for silken cats to slip under

. . . and hollyhocks to gossip over.

The
brilliant
disarray
of autumn
blurs some
lines . . .

12

. . . while
it sharpens
others in
the garden
geometry of
Williamsburg.

Catalpa trees along the Palace Green, seedpods dangling from their newly barren branches, frame a latticework view of autumn's fading colors.

THE CAPITOL

"What a temptation to sit in silence and let the past speak to us of those great patriots whose voices once resounded in these halls, and whose farseeing wisdom, high courage, and unselfish devotion to the common good will ever be an inspiration to noble living."
—*JOHN D. ROCKEFELLER, JR.*

To attentive ears the echoes of stirring events resound again in the Hall of the House of Burgesses, reconstructed on the site of Patrick Henry's "Caesar-Brutus" speech and his defiant resolutions opposing the Stamp Act; of George Mason's Virginia Declaration of Rights; the May 15, 1776, Resolution for Independence, which led directly to Philadelphia and the July 4 Declaration; the pioneering Virginia constitution of that same year, model for many other states; and the introduction of Thomas Jefferson's famous Statute for Religious Freedom.

Contrasting with the austerity of the Hall of the House of Burgesses, luxury characterizes the Council Chamber. The upper house of colonial Virginia's legislature, the Council was an appointive body. Members selected from among the colony's landed aristocracy served at the behest of the crown. Quite a few, nevertheless—like the Nelsons of Yorktown and John Page of Rosewell—ardently supported independence and paid dearly for it.

The General Court, highest judicial tribunal in the colony, met twice yearly here in the Capitol. Civil cases occupied most of its attention, but criminal offenses punishable by mutilation or death also came before it. In this setting the fifteen survivors of Blackbeard's pirate crew faced trial, thirteen of them being sentenced to hang for their crimes.

Framed by massive candlesticks, portraits of Edmund Pendleton, John Robinson, and Patrick Henry—each a power in the political life of Virginia—lend dignity to the Conference Room of the Capitol. Here councillors and burgesses met to conduct morning prayer and to resolve legislative differences between their two houses.

A likeness of Elizabeth I, painted by Marcus Geerarts the Elder about 1585, dominates the Secretary's office in the Capitol.

This portrait of the Duke of Gloucester hangs outside the Council chamber. The only one of Queen Anne's eighteen children to survive infancy, young Prince William died in 1700 at the age of eleven.

ERECTED to provide an appropriate official residence for the king's deputy, the Palace housed five lieutenant governors and two governors, from Alexander Spotswood, the soldier-architect who supervised its construction, to John Murray, Earl of Dunmore, whose flight to the safety of a warship in the York River ended British rule in Virginia. The Palace also served as the executive mansion for Patrick Henry and Thomas Jefferson, the first and second elected governors of the Commonwealth of Virginia.

Opposite page:
The display of swords, pistols, and muskets in the entrance hall symbolizes the authority and might of the British crown and the long continuity of governance here.

The pantry served as a storeroom and as an office where the governor's butler kept accounts and exercised strict control over the wine and liquor inventory and the valuable plate. According to the inventory taken in 1770 after the death of Norborne Berkeley, Baron de Botetourt, the penultimate royal governor, over 1,600 items including silver and glass were stored in the pantry.

The front parlor was used as a waiting room, a place of business, and a setting for polite entertainment. Visitors waiting to see the governor could contemplate and admire the set of "scripture prints" that adorn the walls. Governor Dunmore originally owned the unusual silver candelabrum.

The dining room served both as a place to eat and as a place of business. In the eighteenth century an important meal might have included several courses, each featuring a variety of dishes often arranged symmetrically. An elaborate dessert course concluded the dinner. The painted canvas floorcloth was a fashionable and attractive form of floor covering of the time.

Opposite page:
Acoustically superb and elegant in decor, the Palace ballroom again resounds on appropriate occasions with sprightly airs of colonial days. Jacob Kirckman of London made the double keyboard harpsichord in 1762. The extremely elegant portraits of George III and his consort, Queen Charlotte, are by Allan Ramsay, the king's official portrait painter.

The powder room contains the "1 Wig block with Screw Stands" listed in the Botetourt inventory. Its use as a wig dressing room was probably a fashionable innovation of his lordship's.

Ornamental arrangements of arms and globe lamps decorate the passage that leads to the staircase.

The royal governor frequently conducted official business in the middle room upstairs where his Council, the embodiment of tradition in the colony, often met. Crimson damask, elegant looking glasses, and mahogany furniture bespeak the room's ceremonial character.

Summer calls for green silk gauze mosquito curtains on the antique Virginia bed in his lordship's bedchamber. Lord Botetourt probably purchased the mahogany bedstead from the estate of his predecessor, Lieutenant Governor Francis Fauquier.

Spring raindrops blur the view of the Palace gates and the green beyond.

Food for the royal governor's table was prepared in a kitchen separate from the Palace itself. Lavish hospitality was expected of the crown's representative as Governor Botetourt noted in 1769: "Fifty two dined with me yesterday, and I expect at least that number today."

Opposite page:

BRUTON PARISH CHURCH

BRUTON PARISH was formed in 1674 by the merger of two earlier parishes. The present church, designed by Governor Spotswood, was completed in 1715 and a tower was added in 1769. It has been in continuous use since the days when church and state in Virginia were united and this edifice represented the established Anglican authority in the colony.

THE COURTHOUSE

ON July 26, 1776, the Declaration of Independence was proclaimed to the people of Williamsburg from the steps of this building. It has stood here on Market Square for two centuries, housing—until 1932—both the municipal court of Williamsburg and the court of James City County. County courts in colonial times were the principal agents of local government in Virginia, exercising executive as well as judicial powers.

THE WREN BUILDING

THE oldest academic building in English America, the Wren Building dominates the College of William and Mary yard. Its foundation was laid in 1695.

Here in the Common Room the professors could relax, and valuable "philosophic" apparatus could be kept safely out of students' reach.

The master of the Grammar School and his chief usher prepared boys of twelve to sixteen for college. They taught Latin, Greek, mathematics, and penmanship, and their discipline was strict.

TIIE POWDER MAGAZINE
and GUARDHOUSE

THE Magazine, built in 1715, held the colony's military equipment and gunpowder. As tempers rose in 1775, Governor Dunmore thought it prudent to remove the powder from patriot reach. His surreptitious attempt was discovered—and that spark ignited the tinder of revolution in Virginia.

THE PUBLIC GAOL

THE Public Gaol (pronounced "jail") stands today as grim evidence of crime and punishment in colonial America. Debtors and common criminals sometimes languished for months inside this "strong, sweet Prison." Completed in 1704, after the Revolution the gaol served as the city jail of Williamsburg until 1910.

HOMES and GARDENS

In accord with the city's basic law, Williamsburg building lots were capacious: half an acre each. The law also required that they be fenced.

JAMES GEDDY HOUSE and FOUNDRY

JAMES GEDDY and his sons were successful local craftsmen. James the elder was a gunsmith and brass founder. His sons David and William took over when he died, offering their services in the "Gun-Smith's, Cutler's, and Founder's Trades." Apparently they did blacksmithing and farriery, too. James the younger became one of the town's foremost silversmiths. Extensive archaeological excavation of the property has turned up artifacts from all of these trades.

In the front bedroom of the Geddy House a desk cluttered with writing materials and toilet articles emphasizes that any room in a small colonial home might serve several functions.

Opposite page
Molten metal never fails to provide a spectacular display of sparks and fumes in the Geddy foundry.

GEORGE WYTHE HOUSE

THIS was the home of a distinguished Virginian whose public career
spanned a decisive half-century in American life. One of the foremost
classical scholars in the colonies, George Wythe befriended a young student
at the College of William and Mary, Thomas Jefferson, who later studied law
in Wythe's office and referred to him as "my faithful and beloved Mentor in
youth, and my most affectionate friend through life." John Marshall, too,
studied under him. Wythe was a close friend of royal governors Fauquier
and Botetourt, a burgess, speaker of the House of Delegates, a judge, the
first professor of law in an American college—at William and Mary—and a
signer of the Declaration of Independence.

A symmetrical garden plan divides the property behind the Wythe House into distinct areas. In the service yard are a smokehouse, kitchen, laundry, stable, and other outbuildings. Opposite are the orchard and kitchen garden.

The pleasure garden is lined with tree box topiary and ends in an arbor of hornbeam.

The study

The parlor

The dining room

The student's room

In the southeast bedroom (*above*) blue and white resist has been used for curtains and bed and chair coverings. All of the pieces in the southwest bedroom (*below*) are of eighteenth-century American origin except the mahogany basin stand (English, about 1770).

WETHERBURN'S TAVERN

HENRY WETHERBURN owned or managed several of Williamsburg's most famous eighteenth-century taverns, sometimes more than one at a time. When he bought this property in 1738, he was already host at the Raleigh. An inventory of his possessions, some of them doubtless acquired in his successive marriages to the widows of other innkeepers, has proved most helpful in refurnishing the tavern to its former state.

George Washington often dined or supped at Southall's, as the tavern was known in his day. Since most of the flooring is original, one may actually walk here in Washington's footsteps.

Opposite page:
Afternoon sunlight bathes the spire of Bruton Parish Church, which overlooks Mr. Wythe's garden and stable yard.

Mr. Wetherburn's inventory listed nineteen beds, indicating that he could put up for the night as many as thirty-eight persons, counting two per bed.

A variety of foods could be found in the tavern's busy kitchen.

From the paddock behind a small vegetable garden are visible the back of the smokehouse, the dairy, and a corner of the kitchen, with the wellhead and the rear of the tavern itself showing between them.

BRUSH-EVERARD HOUSE

JOHN BRUSH, gunsmith, built the front portion of this simple home in 1717. It contains touches of elegance, however, such as the carvings that dress the central stairway. The most prominent of many later owners, Thomas Everard served as clerk of York County from 1745 until his death in 1784. He was also auditor of Virginia and was elected mayor of Williamsburg in 1766. Appropriate to Everard's status and aspirations, a collection of books has been placed in the library; the titles are those listed by Thomas Jefferson in 1771 for the guidance of a young planter.

The dining room

The northeast bedroom

The parlor

The library

Two views of the
southwest bedroom

Opposite page:
The gardener's workshop

The northwest bedroom

RALEIGH TAVERN

THIS most famous of Williamsburg taverns was dedicated to Sir Walter Raleigh, who took a leading part in sending colonists to the New World. A lead bust of him adorns the main doorway. The Raleigh was a center for social and business activity and the scene of many public auctions of land, slaves, and goods. On at least two occasions the governor dissolved the House of Burgesses; the legislators reassembled here to decide on policies and actions in opposition to those of king and Parliament.

Patrons of the public dining room could expect plain fare served—at regulated prices—on sturdy dishes of pewter and salt-glazed stoneware.

Besides keeping his own records, the innkeeper served as postmaster to both transients and townspeople. The ribbons tacked criss-cross to the wall held messages waiting to be claimed.

A blazing fire adds warmth and an air of hospitality to the barroom.

Players and onlookers alike betted heavily on the outcome of a game in the Raleigh's billiard room. The great table was made in England in 1738.

PEYTON RANDOLPH HOUSE

LIKE his father, Sir John Randolph, Peyton Randolph was a distinguished lawyer, an influential political leader, and speaker of the House of Burgesses. In that office from 1766 to 1775 and as president of the First Continental Congress in Philadelphia, he wielded enormous power in the struggle for American independence—generally on behalf of moderation. Comte de Rochambeau, commander of French forces in the siege of Yorktown, made his headquarters here while preparing for that battle.

The beautiful oak paneling of this bedroom is unique in Williamsburg.

In Peyton Randolph's comfortable library, the
floor is covered with a painted floorcloth.
Randolph's books, bought from his estate by
Thomas Jefferson, became with Jefferson's
own volumes the nucleus of the Library of
Congress.

Opposite page:
The spacious center passage and
stairs were characteristic of large
colonial Virginia homes.

The special character
of colonial Virginia
architecture . . .

becomes evident
in the homes and in
the outbuildings.

Behind the Waters Storehouse and
the Printing Office.

Ever so briefly, the city
feels winter's frosty touch.

The Greenhow
Brick Office.

Opposite page:
The St. George
Tucker House.

THE CRAFTS

In the eighteenth century most gentlemen wore wigs made to measure by the wigmaker. Virginians wore powdered wigs on formal occasions; for everyday use a man chose whatever color he liked. Although some shops accepted female trade, most Virginia women kept their own hair and dressed it at home.

An imposing array of elixirs and ointments, medicinal herbs, aromatic spices, and leeches greets visitors to the Pasteur & Galt Apothecary Shop. Most eighteenth-century apothecaries prescribed and dispensed medicine and fulfilled the role of surgeon as occasion demanded.

The sign of the Golden Ball identifies the shop where James Craig, master silversmith and jeweler, practiced his exacting trade in colonial days.

A communications and graphic arts center for the Virginia colony, the printing office combined the functions of a newspaper printing office, book bindery, stationery store, and post office. Today the printer once more pulls the bar of his ancient press to produce accurate reproductions of early printing.

The bookbinder skillfully fashions elegant bindings from supple leathers, embellishing them with hand-tooled designs.

Baskets woven of oak splints take many shapes and sizes. They are strong, light in weight, and long lasting.

Horses were as common in Virginia then as automobiles are today. The saddler and harnessmaker practiced an important craft in the community.

Every colonial home and farm needed items from the black-
smith's forge—shoes for horses and oxen, tools, andirons, hinges,
locks, and so on.

The weaver produces
fine homespun fabrics
in attractive patterns.

Opposite page:
A scarecrow keeps watch over the
cornfield by Robertson's Windmill,
a post mill of a type well known
on the Virginia peninsula in the
eighteenth century.

Casks of various shapes and sizes were the shipping containers for many eighteenth-century goods, wet and dry, crude or manufactured.

The bootmaker fashions his footwear by hand on wooden lasts. He also makes pitch-coated leather jacks for beer or ale, leather dice cups, buckets, and other items.

The gunsmith makes and repairs the locks, stocks, and barrels of all kinds of firearms.

Boards and beams for an eighteenth-century Virginia home were often produced by hand with a two-man pit saw. The log was mounted over a saw pit dug into the ground. One sawyer stood underneath while the other stationed himself on top of the log as they worked the huge saw down its length.

"Black love ribands," "Sleeve Knots," "stuff Shoes for Ladies," "Cloaks and Cardinals"—such were the frills, finery, and necessities sold by Margaret Hunter and her sister Jane in their shop on Duke of Gloucester Street.

The musical instrument maker (*right*) in his shop next to the cabinetmaker, the music teacher (*below*) in his room on Duke of Gloucester Street, and performers of many kinds testify that the sound of music is as important today as it was in colonial times.

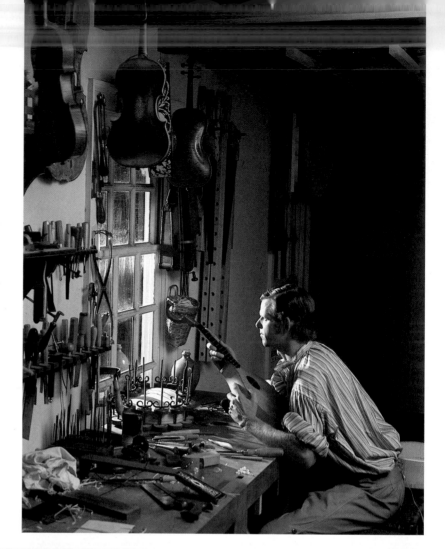

Above:
In camp, in training, or in the field, fifers and drummers were essential to eighteenth-century army routine. They provided the everyday sounds of a soldier's life from reveille to tattoo, improved morale and discipline, and directed and inspired the troops in battle. The Fifes and Drums of Colonial Williamsburg play martial music of the revolutionary period.

Below:
The militiamen of the Virginia State Garrison Regiment drill and fire revolutionary-era muskets.

KING'S ARMS TAVERN

IN the days of William Byrd III, King's Arms was one of the best-known taverns in the city of Williamsburg. During the Revolution its proprietress, Mrs. Jane Vobe, supplied food and drink to American troops, and Baron von Steuben, drillmaster of the Continental Army, was a regular patron. Today it specializes in traditional southern foods served in the hospitable atmosphere of another age.

Twentieth-century visitors may dine like their colonial forebears. Service is provided by "young Gentlemen of the College of William and Mary."

Today's bountiful fare of King's Arms Tavern.

CHOWNING'S TAVERN

AN alehouse typical of the colonial period, Josiah Chowning's Tavern served a less sophisticated clientele. In the tradition of that earlier day, Chowning's offers simple, hearty fare to its twentieth-century patrons.

"Gambols"—colonial games, music, entertainment, and various "diversions"—take place nightly at Chowning's Tavern.

CHRISTIANA CAMPBELL'S TAVERN

CONVENIENT to the Capitol and noted for good food, this popular hostelry attracted many prominent leaders of the Virginia colony. George Washington and some of his friends had a club here. Mrs. Campbell, the proprietress, was acknowledged to be a fine hostess. Today Mrs. Campbell's tavern once more operates in the spirit of its eighteenth-century mistress.

COLONIAL WILLIAMSBURG

IN 1926, inspired by the foresight and enthusiasm of Dr. W. A. R. Goodwin, then rector of Bruton Parish Church, Mr. John D. Rockefeller, Jr., became interested in the preservation and restoration of eighteenth-century Williamsburg, and thereafter devoted his personal attention and resources to the fulfillment of this goal.

The purpose of Colonial Williamsburg, in the words of the Board of Trustees, is "to re-create accurately the environment of the men and women of eighteenth-century Williamsburg and to bring about such an understanding of their lives and times that present and future generations may more vividly appreciate the contribution of these early Americans to the ideals and culture of our country."

Today, the Historic Area of Colonial Williamsburg embraces about 175 acres, the heart of the old city. Eighty-eight original eighteenth- and early nineteenth-century structures still stand. Several main buildings and many outbuildings that did not survive the years have been reconstructed on their original foundations after extensive archaeological investigation and historical research. Also, ninety acres of colorful gardens and greens have been re-created using many plants known to the eighteenth-century colonists.